Religious Education and the Law:

A Catechist Handbook

Mary Angela Shaughnessy, SCN

npcd

An initiative of the National Association of Parish Coordinators and Directors of Religious Education (NPCD) of the National Catholic Educational Association (NCEA), Department of Religious Education.

Cover and text design: Beatriz Ruiz
Editorial assistance: Cecelia Edwards
Publication assistance: Phyllis Kokus

Copies can be ordered from:
NCEA, Publications and Sales
1077 30th Street NW
Washington DC 20007-3852
202-337-6232
202-333-6706 (fax)

ISBN 1-55833-175-1
6th Printing 2000

Dedication

This work is dedicated to the Sisters of Charity of Nazareth who have labored since 1812 to serve in the ministry of religious education.

About the Author

Sister Mary Angela Shaughnessy is a Sister of Charity of Nazareth who has taught at all levels of Catholic education from elementary through graduate school. She served eight years as principal of a Catholic high school. She holds a bachelor's degree in English and a master's degree in education from Spalding University, a master's degree in English and a JD degree in law from the University of Louisville, and a Ph.D. in educational administration and supervision from Boston College. She is an adjunct professor in Boston College's Catholic School Leadership Program and in the University of San Francisco's Institute for Catholic Educational Leadership. Currently, Sister Mary Angela is Professor of Education and University Counsel at Spalding University. A frequent lecturer at NCEA conventions, she is the author of nine NCEA texts and the recipient of the 1991 NCEA Secondary Department Award. She is a member of the bar in the state of Kentucky.

Contents

Preface

Today more than ever before lay persons are being asked to share in the catechetical ministry of the Church by serving as catechetical leaders, catechists, and religious education board members.

This handbook is designed to provide essential information concerning civil law and its impact on Church institutions and programs. It is not intended as specific legal advice. If legal advice is needed, the services of a competent attorney licensed in your state should be sought.

The information in this volume is arranged in four parts. Each section offers basic legal background to support your ministerial perspective. Part 1 covers issues related to your professionalism as a catechist in your privileged role as a partner in handing on the faith. Part 2 is concerned with issues relating to your direct contact with students. Part 3 addresses two of the basic administrative issues that impact you directly as a catechist.

This volume is designed to be used in a variety of settings. Throughout, the term catechist is used in the classic sense to designate the person responsible for working directly with adults, children and youth in the ministry of helping them toward a greater understanding of their faith. For purposes of simplicity, the term "catechetical leader" is used as an inclusive term meant to designate the person accountable for the direction, coordination and/or administration of the diverse responsibilities within a parish offering catechetical, educational and formational programs. In the application of the information covered and its relevance to diverse parish ministries, the term "catechetical leader" can also be read to apply to youth ministers, deacons, those in formation ministries and others in parish leadership roles whose titles are too diverse to enumerate.

Designed as a helpful resource, this handbook is offered in the spirit of St. Thomas More who once observed, "It is a question of love, not law." May this be a useful tool for you in your role as a minister of God's love — protecting and ensuring the safety of all whom you serve in Jesus' name.

Barbara F. Campbell, D. Min.
Associate Executive Director
NCEA, Department of Religious Education

Part 1:
Legal Issues and the Professionalism of Catechists

TOPIC 1

Religious Education and the US Constitution

The United States Constitution protects persons from arbitrary governmental deprivation of their constitutional freedoms. Persons in Catholic educational and catechetical programs, however, cannot claim such protections because their programs are in private institutions administered by private persons.

The bottom line is that when one enters a private institution such as a parish, one voluntarily surrenders the protections of the Constitution. A catechist or student can always leave the program or parish, but so long as the person remains in the institution, constitutional protections are not available. Thus, a religious education program does not have to accept behaviors about which the public sector has no choice and is even required to protect.

What cannot lawfully done in the public sector may be done in a religious education program. For example, the First Amendment to the U.S. Constitution protects persons' 'rights to free speech' therefore, administrators in public schools may not make rules prohibiting the expression of an unpopular viewpoint.

Since no such constitutional protection exists in the private sector, catechetical leaders may restrict the speech of both students and catechists. A religious education program could ban pro-choice statements, for example.

Fairness and Due Process

Religious education programs, while not bound to grant constitutional freedoms *per se,* are bound to act in a manner characterized by fairness. Some legal experts talk about a "smell" test. If an action "smells" wrong when a person examines it, it may be suspect. For example, if a catechist were to tell a student and her parents, "You are dismissed from the class, and I am not giving you a reason," an objective observer would probably find that the action "smells" wrong. Persons do have rights, even if not grounded in the Constitution, to be treated fairly; dismissing a student and refusing to give a reason do not seem to constitute fairness.

It is not uncommon for parents, students, or staff to claim that their constitutional rights have been violated in a religious education program when, in fact, no constitutional rights ever existed in the first place. These realities need to be clarified very early in the relationship between a parish religious education program and its catechists, parents, and students. One way that prevents possible misunderstandings is the use of comprehensive handbooks which outline the rights and responsibilities of all persons in parish religious education programs. Catechists must familiarize themselves with handbooks and must implement program policies in their sessions.

Parents and Students as Contracting Parties

Religious education is a right of all parishioners, but it is not an absolute right. It is possible for a young person or an adult to behave in such a manner that the right is forfeited. The parish, in effect, enters into a contract with the parents of young people. The parish agrees to provide religious education and the parents agree to see that their children come to classes or activities and behave in an appropriate manner. It is advisable to put the contractual understanding in writing and to have both parents and young persons sign the agreement, if possible.

Breach of contract occurs when one party fails to perform. When a parish is involved in litigation with personnel or members, the court will examine the provisions of the contract.

There are virtually no cases in courts of record involving allegations of church failure to provide religious education to young persons. However, the present state of litigation certainly leads one to expect that such litigation may be forthcoming.

The use of religious education handbooks and the requirement that parents and young persons sign an agreement that they "have read and agree to abide by the provisions of the handbook," will do much to ensure an effective program and compliance with reasonable rules and regulations.

TOPIC 2

Negligence and the Catechist: What Is Legal Liability?

If a catechist is sued, chances are that the suit will allege negligence. In assessing whether a person's behavior is negligent, a court will use the "reasonable person test" : would a "reasonable person" [catechist] in the defendant's situation have acted in this manner?

Religious education programs present many possible negligence situations. It must be frankly stated that the religious education program presents more legal risks than does the average classroom. When students are not in the ordinary classroom setting, it may well be more difficult to ensure that students understand and abide by rules and regulations.

Four Elements

There are four elements which must be present before legal negligence can be found: *duty, violation of duty, proximate cause, and injury*. If any one of these elements is missing, legal negligence cannot be present.

Duty

The person charged with negligence must have had a *duty* in the situation. Catechists are not responsible for injuries occurring at a place where or a time when they had no responsibility. But within the religious education setting, students have a right to safety and catechetical leaders and catechists have a duty to protect the safety of all those entrusted to their care. Catechetical leaders have a duty to develop and implement rules and regulations guiding catechists in providing for student safety. Catechists have a duty to ensure that those guidelines are followed.

Violation of duty

Negligence cannot exist if the second element, *violation of duty*, is not present. Courts understand that accidents and spontaneous actions can occur. If a catechist is properly supervising students during a break and one student picks up an object, throws it, and thus injures another student, the catechist is not responsible. However, if a catechist who is responsible for supervision were to allow object throwing to continue without attempting to stop it and a student were injured, the catechist would probably be found to have violated a duty.

Proximate cause

The violation of duty must be the *proximate cause* of the injury. The court or jury has to decide whether proper supervision could have prevented the injury and, in so deciding, the court has to look at the facts of each individual case. In determining proximate cause, the concept of foreseeability is important. Would a reasonable person foresee that there is a likelihood of injury? Catechists should periodically examine their instructional sites for hazards.

Injury

The fourth element necessary for a finding of negligence is *injury*. No matter how irresponsible the behavior of an educator, there is no legal negligence if there is no injury. Injuries do not have to be physical. They can be psychological, mental, or emotional as well.

The best protection for a catechist against being accused of negligence is a reasonable effort to implement rules and regulations.

TOPIC 3

To Copy or Not To Copy: That Is the Question

Most catechists realize that copyright law exists. However, it is not uncommon to find catechists copying such items as workbooks, other consumable materials and/or large portions of books and print materials.

Upon reflection, most educators would agree that copyright protection is a just law. Persons who create materials are entitled to the fruits of their labors. Those who use an author's creations without paying royalties, buying copies or seeking permission are guilty of stealing.

What Is Fair Use?

Section 107 of the 1976 Copyright Act deals with "fair use" and specifically states that the fair use of copies in teaching "is not an infringement of copyright."

The "sticking point" is what the term "fair use" means. Four factors to be included in any determination of fair use:

- the purpose and character of the use, including whether such use is of a commercial nature or is for nonprofit educational purposes
- the nature of the copyrighted work
- the amount and substantiality of the portion used in relation to the copyrighted work as a whole
- the effect of the use upon the potential market for or value of the copyrighted work.

Guidelines

A congressional committee developed *Guidelines for Classroom Copying in Not-for-Profit Educational Institutions,* printed in House Report 94-1476, 94th Congress 2d Sess. (1976). Although these guidelines do not have the force of law that the statute has, judges do use them in deciding cases. Some examples of the guidelines follow.

For poetry, copying of a complete poem of less than 250 words printed on no more than two pages or of an excerpt of 250 words from a longer poem is allowed. For prose, a complete work of less than 2,500 words or an excerpt from a longer work of not more than 1,000 words or 10% of the work is permissible. The guidelines mandate that copying meet this test of *brevity*.

The copying must be *spontaneous*. The educator must have decided more or less on the spur of the moment to use an item.

A last requirement is that the copying must not have a *cumulative effect*. Videotapes may be kept for 45 days only. During the first 10 days, a catechist may use the tape once in a class (although there is a provision for one repetition for legitimate instructional review.) For the remaining 35 days catechists may use the tape for evaluative purposes only.

As many legal authorities have observed, copyright violation is stealing. It appears, then, that "Thou shalt not steal" remains good law.

TOPIC 4

Child Abuse Laws and the Catechist

One of the most serious issues confronting educators today is child abuse. Children and adolescents often choose catechists as confidantes in their struggles to deal with abuse and its effects.

Statutory Considerations

All fifty states have laws requiring educators to report suspected abuse and/or neglect. Statutes generally mandate reporting procedures. The reporting individual usually makes a phone report which is followed by a written report within a specified time period, often 48 hours. The law usually mandates that a person who knew of child abuse or neglect and failed to report it can be fined and/or charged with a misdemeanor or felony.

Defining Abuse

What is child abuse? How much corporal punishment is too

much? Who makes the final determination? Can what one person considers abuse be considered valid parental corporal punishment by another? Are there any allowances for differing cultural practices? These and other issues are addressed by local guidelines, guidelines that catechists are responsible to be aware of.

Reporting Abuse

As a mandated reporter, the catechist's function is to present information that leads to the reasonable suspicion that abuse has occurred. Appropriate officials will determine whether the report should be investigated further or simply "screened out" as a well-intentioned report that does not appear to be in the category of abuse.

Allegations Against Educators

The number of cases alleging teacher or other educational employee abuse of children is increasing.

Any student or parent complaint alleging abuse by a staff member must be thoroughly investigated. Failure to do so can put the parish and its officials at grave legal risk. Catechists who receive reports alleging abuse by other catechists or staff members must notify the catechetical leader or appropriate authority.

Policies and Guidelines

Pastors, catechetical leaders, and boards of education adopt policies governing reporting child abuse/neglect and investigating allegations of abuse by staff *before* the need for such policies surfaces. It is preferable to have a policy that is never needed than to have no policy and be forced to try to construct one when faced with a need. Catechists must be aware of all relevant policies, guidelines and the necessary forms and procedures.

TOPIC 5

Sexual Harassment: What Is It? What Does It Mean for Religious Education?

Catechists should understand what sexual harassment is. Federal anti-discrimination law can bind Catholic institutions.

Definition

The Equal Employment Opportunities Commission has issued guidelines which define sexual harassment, forbidden by Title VII as:

> Unwelcomed sexual advances, requests for sexual favors, and other verbal or physical conduct of a sexual nature when:

- Submission to such conduct by an individual is made explicitly or implicitly a term of employment;
- Submission to, or rejection of such conduct by an individual is used as the basis for an employment decision;
- And such conduct has the purpose or effect to interfere with an individual's work performance, or creates a hostile or intimidating environment.

The above definition concerns employment conditions; however, "education" can be substituted for "employment" in the definitions, and the basis for Title IX violations would be evident.

It appears that if Title IX applies to the Catholic school (and no case to date has held that it does not), students are protected against sexual harassment in much the same manner that employees are protected. Since religious education programs are sponsored by parishes in much the same manner as schools are sponsored, it seems that participants should also be protected from sexual harassment.

Examples

The following are examples of behaviors that could constitute sexual harassment: sexual proposition, off-color jokes, inappropriate physical contact, innuendoes, sexual offers, looks, and gestures.

Prevention

It is far easier to prevent claims of sexual harassment than it is to defend them. To that end, employees, catechists, and volunteers should participate in some kind of in-service training that raises awareness of sexual harassment and other gender issues. Staff members must understand what sorts of behaviors can be construed as sexual harassment.

Catechists should discuss issues of fair treatment of others with their students, and should promptly correct any students who demean others. Defenses such as, "I was only kidding," will not be accepted if the alleged victim states that the behavior was offensive and unwelcome and a court finds that a reasonable person could find the behavior offensive and unwelcome.

Sexual harassment and other forms of demeaning behavior have no place in a catechetical program. Guarding the dignity of all members of the parish community should be a priority for all catechists and catechetical leaders.

TOPIC 6

AIDS, Blood-borne Pathogens and Other Diseases

The word, AIDS, evokes many emotions: fear, compassion, pity and anxiety, to name a few. Today's catechists are no strangers to these emotions. It is not surprising that catechists, like other educators, have questions and concerns about AIDS and other blood-borne diseases.

Catechist Responsibilities

The standard which determines catechists' duty in any situation involving young people is the "reasonable person" standard. The fact-finder in a court case must determine whether the catechist acted as a reasonable person in the catechist's position would act.

A catechist has a higher responsibility to students than a stranger would have to them. There is a good possibility that a judge or jury would not accept "fear of coming in contact with blood" as a reason for a catechist to decline to protect students.

Universal precautions should always be used when dealing with any situation involving body fluids. Even if catechists knew that certain students were HIV positive, there is no guarantee that other students are HIV negative. Persons who are HIV positive may not know that they are.

Currently, medical experts suggest that it can take two weeks to six months before one tests positive for the HIV virus, and up to 10 years before symptoms appear.

Thus, the prudent approach is to assume that everyone *may* be infected and to take universal precautions when dealing with body fluids. Every catechist and staff member should have gloves and disinfectant within easy access, and all should participate in the in-service training offered in this area.

Recommendations

1. Remember that everyone, including people with AIDS, are protected against discrimination.
2. Remember that everyone has privacy rights. Medical information is confidential and only those with a legal right to know can be informed.
3. Assume that any staff member or student may be HIV positive or may have a communicable disease.
4. Do not discuss the physical, psychological, mental or emotional condition of any student with anyone except parents and/or those the parents designate.
5. Attitudes are important and can be expressed as much by actions as by words.
6. Educators and other professionals are held to a higher standard than are "ordinary" people.
7. Practice universal precautions.

The fear of AIDS is real. It is the task of catechists to model Christian behavior and values. The question that should always be asked is: what would Jesus do if he were here?

Part 2:
Legal Issues and the Responsibilities of Catechists

TOPIC 1

Student Rights and Catechist Responsibilities: An Approach To Healthy Discipline

Catechists and catechetical leaders face the challenge of respecting student rights while upholding discipline and order. Common law and common sense indicate that persons and institutions responsible for the education of children and youth are expected to hold students to standards of behavior. The main source of law governing the private institution is contract law.

Student Rights

Although not protected by the Constitution, Catholic students and parents have property rights in the contract between the parent and the parish. Courts can consider parent and or/student handbooks or similar documents as conferring property rights. Failure to protect the reputation of students can result in defamation liability in the Catholic parish in the same way such a failure can result in constitutional violation of liberty interests in the public sector. Catechists should naturally be concerned with protecting the good name of all entrusted to their care. Disciplinary procedures, records, etc., may impact a student's reputation. Care must be taken to guard against unnecessary harm.

Catechist Responsibilities

In meeting the requirements of fairness, catechists should ask themselves these questions: What are our disciplinary procedures? Are they reasonable? Are all young people treated fairly and, as far as reasonably possible, in the same way? Is there a clear procedure that young persons and parents can expect will be followed?

Most education officials and attorneys would agree that the best education law is, like medicine, preventive. The best defense is having tried to follow the right course in the first place. Catechists and administrators must realize that, despite their best efforts in any and all areas of religious education, they may face lawsuits.

Catechetical leaders and catechists must understand that it is impossible to identify everything a student might do that could result in suspension or expulsion.

The beginning point for rules development is the parish or program philosophy. Harsh policies and procedures have no place in a religious education program. Allowances must be made for the needs of young people. The guiding principle in any consideration of student rights and discipline should be the desire to act in a Christian manner characterized by fairness and compassion.

TOPIC 2

Search and Seizure and Other Issues of Privacy

The privacy rights of persons are treasured. One of the privileges of living in the United States is the right to be free of unreasonable governmental or other intrusion into the private affairs of persons. One main concern in this area is that presented by the issue of search and seizure.

The Fourth Amendment to the United States Constitution protects the right of persons to be secure in their persons and property. The Fourth Amendment does not apply to private institutions, such as Catholic schools and religious education programs. Nonetheless, program administrators should have some kind of policy for searching students and/or seizing their possessions. Searching a student should require "more" cause than searching a desk or a locker.

Lockers and Desks

Lockers and desks are parish property and the catechetical leader and catechists have every right to examine them and their contents. A religious education program strengthens its position with students and parents by including in the parent/student handbook a phrase such as, "The parish is co-tenant of lockers and desks and reserves the right to search them at any time without notice."

"Search" Situations

If a catechetical leader or catechist believes that a young person is carrying a dangerous item on his or her person, the catechist should ask the student for it. If it is possible to contact the catechetical leader or other administrator, the catechist should do so before beginning a search.

While constitutional protections do not apply, religious education programs and their personnel can be subject to *tort* suits of assault and battery and/or invasion of privacy if a student is harmed because of an unreasonable search. Following the carefully developed diocesan/parish policies and procedures should guide any search and seizure. A common sense "balancing test" should be applied in each case: is this search and its possible effects worth finding whatever it is that staff members are seeking?

Records and Privacy

An issue related to invasion of privacy is confidentiality of records. The content of student files should be released only to authorized persons. Even catechists should be given access to files only for appropriate program-related reasons. Parental signatures should be required before records are sent to anyone.

Non-Custodial Parents

The issue of the non-custodial parent is a significant one

today when so many students are not in the custody of both parents. It is this writer's opinion that religious education programs, like Catholic schools, should voluntarily comply with the law. If one chooses not to comply, one runs the risk of becoming a test case in the courts.

While religious education programs are not held to the constitutional standards that public programs are, all catechists should be concerned with protecting the rights of young people entrusted to their care.

TOPIC 3

Community Service Programs and Other Off-site Activities

Part of the mission of the Catholic parish is to teach service. The philosophies of most religious education programs clearly state that one of the goals of Catholic education is to develop persons who consider service to others a primary responsibility. To that end, many religious education programs have initiated service requirements. These programs may range from preschool and kindergarten students visiting nursing homes at Christmas or adopting a nursing home resident as a grandparent, to sophisticated programs at the high school level involving daily or weekly service at an off-site location. Service programs, and other off-site activities, raise special legal issues.

Parent Awareness and Permission

The family handbook is a good place to provide initial parent notification of the existence of a mandatory student service program. Catechetical leaders should require that all parents sign a statement, such as, "We have read and agree to be governed by this handbook," prior to their children's attending sessions. It can then be presumed that the parents have read the handbook. Catechists often have a role in making sure that all appropriate forms have been gathered and submitted to the catechetical leader.

Parents should also be required to sign a permission slip authorizing student participation. The permission slip should state *where* the student is providing the service, and should state *who* is responsible for providing transportation. While some few parishes may transport students in parish vehicles, most parishes require that students or parents provide transportation. Catechist assistance is vital to ensure that established procedures are followed.

Essential Precautions

It is highly advisable that the supervisor of the service program visit all sites where students will be performing service. Such visits constitute appropriate diligence on the part of the parish.

Particularly if the service program involves released time from religious education, the supervisor should make spot checks of sites to ensure that students are in attendance and acting appropriately. If the sheer numbers and times of the service opportunities preclude such checks, the supervisor should be in regular phone contact with the site supervisor to ascertain that students are in attendance and that program objectives are being met.

The cooperation and support of catechists involved in service programs and other off-site activities is essential to ensuring that all appropriate and necessary precautions are implemented.

TOPIC 4

Athletics and Other Types of Physical Activities

Athletics and other physical activities, including simple play, pose legal concerns for all educational administrators, catechists and catechetical leaders are no exception. With careful planning and the development of clear policies and regulations, physical activity can be a rewarding experience within the religious education program.

Standards of Care

Most lawsuits alleging negligence in educational settings occur in the classroom or other instructional areas, since that is where students spend most of their time. Other areas, however, are potentially more dangerous than the classroom. Hence, a greater standard of care will be expected from catechists and administrators. Athletic programs are clearly activities that are more dangerous than normal classroom activities.

Students who participate in organized athletic programs should be given permission slips for their parents to sign. If any parents should refuse to sign the slips, their children should not be allowed to participate.

Negligence Factors

Administrators will not be held responsible for every mistake of adult supervisors, but only for those which a reasonable person could have foreseen. One requirement for legal negligence is *proximate cause*, which is a contributing factor. If a supervising adult were to organize a game in which thirteen year old students played against six year old students and the adult failed to establish and maintain safety measures, that inaction could be the proximate cause of an injury if a six year old were injured by an overzealous thirteen year old.

The court must decide whether proper performance of *duty* could have prevented the injury and, in so doing, the court has to look at the facts of each individual case.

To prevail in a lawsuit, a person must have sustained an *injury* for which the court can award a remedy. Injuries do not have to be physical; they can be emotional or psychological as well.

Even if every possible precaution were taken, the possibility for student injury while participating in sports programs or other physical activity is very high. Administrators have very real duties to ensure that only competent persons are utilized as supervisors. Further, administrators must establish policies for supervisors to follow that provide:

- clear procedures to be followed when accidents occur
- minimal delay in seeking medical attention when needed
- hazard-free equipment and playing areas.

There is no absolute protection against lawsuits, particularly when physical activities are involved. Following established guidelines is an important step in ensuring everyone's protection and safety.

TOPIC 5

Keeping Confidences of Young People: What Can You Tell? What Must You Tell?

One of the more perplexing situations facing catechists today is that presented by student sharing of confidential information. The young persons of the '90s may well face more pressures and problems than the young persons of any other decade. The responsibility for receiving student confidences and advising students in both day-to-day situations and crises can be overwhelming.

None of us can afford to think that we can help all students all the time. We cannot. If a student were to come to a catechist or catechetical leader and tell the adult that he or she is experiencing shortness of breath and chest pain, the adult would quickly summon both the student's parents and medical assistance. Yet, psychological problems are no less serious than physical ones, and the lay person who attempts to deal with such problems unaided may well be courting tragedy for both self and student.

General Norms

Confidentiality is generally held to mean that an individual or individuals will keep private information that has been given to them, and will not reveal it. It is not unheard of for an adult, who would not hesitate to get help for a friend, to believe that a student who is talking about suicide is not serious, or can be talked out of the planned action, or is not capable of carrying out a threatened suicide. As child and adolescent psychologists report, young people do not usually comprehend the finality of death and do not think through the long-term ramifications of a suicide attempt.

If a student tells a catechist that he or she is going to harm self or others, the catechist must reveal that information even if a promise of confidentiality has been given.

It is a widely held myth that counselors, physicians, psychologists, and social workers have legal immunity from responsibility for any injuries that may arise from their not acting on confidential information presented to them. Most states have abolished counselor immunity, and the few who still "have it on the books" have imposed severe limitations on the concept. Counselors and other adults must make it very clear to confiding individuals that they will keep their confidences unless their own health, life or safety or those of another are involved.

Student Journals

Those involved in religious education have long recognized the value of student journal writing. This practice does, however, carry a real risk of student disclosure of information that the adult is compelled to reveal. Catechists must understand that they *are* expected to read what students write. If the catechist cannot read the assignment, then the assignment should not be made. Journal writing has a place in today's religious education curriculum, but adults must be sure that students understand the parameters of the assignment and of the adult's responsibilities of reporting threatened danger.

Retreats and Other Faith Sharing Settings

The retreat experience and other faith sharing opportunities are extremely important for today's Catholic young people. However, students are often at their most vulnerable in such situations. While encouraging students to share, the group leader must once again set the ground rules before the sharing begins.

The wise catechist will establish and enforce ground rules for dealing with student confidences, and will seek help from school officials and/or parents when appropriate.

TOPIC 6

Defamation of Character and the Catechist

"Can I be sued for what I say about a young person?" is a question often asked by catechists who want to do the right thing for students but who want to protect themselves as well. The simple answer to the question is, "Yes, you can be sued."

Definitions

Defamation is a type of *tort*, a civil wrong. Persons who bring defamation suits will have their claims heard in civil, not criminal, courts. Defamation of character involves twin *torts*: slander, which is spoken, and libel, which is written. Defamation is an unprivileged communication, i.e., a statement made by one person to a third party who is not privileged to receive it.

In any educational or ministerial setting, a court might well inquire as to the necessity for the communication. If the communication is found to be unnecessary, even if true, the court could find the individual charged to be in fact guilty of defamation. Some people mistakenly believe that the truth is an absolute defense to defamation. Persons who work with children and adolescents are generally held to a higher standard than is the average adult in a defamation suit.

Any documentation concerning young people must be both accurate and protective of the rights of individuals whose behavior is being described. Records must be objective and factual. Communications should be measured against the standard, "What is written should be specific, behaviorally oriented, and verifiable."

Slander, or oral defamation, can arise in seemingly innocent situations. A catechist risks being accused of slander if negative comments are made about young people to persons who have no right to know.

Cautions for Catechists

Catechists should be extremely prudent in making any comments, whether oral or written, about young people. Comments to parents should be about the parents' own children. Communication should be made only to those persons with a legitimate right to know.

The days when individuals could not see their records are over. In the end, as St. Thomas More once observed, "It is a question of love, not law." If catechists truly care about their students, they will not ask, "How can I write so that I won't get sued?" but will ask, "How can I write so that I protect both the reputation of those in my care and my own reputation as a minister who abides by the highest ethical standards?"

TOPIC 7

Catechist/Student Relationships in Religious Education

Catechists and other staff members care about students. That care extends to all areas of student life. Catechists often find themselves counseling students in personal matters. It is not unusual for a catechist to be placed in the position of "surrogate parent" by a student. Students often entrust catechists with confidential information. Catechists, many of whom have little training in professional counseling, often have questions about what is appropriate in interacting with students outside the classroom and/or parish setting. There are few guidelines available. Catechists and other personnel may find themselves in situations that pose personal and legal risks for the adults as well as the students.

Most educators rightfully consider student confidences to be sacred. If a student confides in a catechist, the student should be able to presume that the confidential information normally will not be shared with anyone. The catechist does not enjoy the type of privilege that doctor/patient, lawyer/client or priest/penitent enjoy. (See also Part 2, Topic 5: Keeping Confidences of Young People.)

Avoiding Allegations of Misconduct

One end of the student/staff relationship spectrum is represented by sexual misconduct. Sexual misconduct *can* be alleged in apparently innocent situations. Students *can* misinterpret touching, and catechists *could* find themselves facing child abuse charges. Extreme caution is in order whenever a catechist touches a student.

Another kind of problem is posed by a student who believes that a catechist has not responded to efforts to achieve a closer relationship. Such a student may accuse a catechist of inappropriate conduct as a retaliatory measure. Catechists must be aware that serious consequences can result from an allegation of child abuse, even if that allegation is eventually proven to be false. At the very least, such a false allegation can be extremely embarrassing for the catechist. To avoid even the slightest hint of impropriety, a catechist should avoid being alone with a single student behind closed doors unless a window or other opening permits outsiders to see into the area. A good question to ask one's self might be, "If this were my child, would I have any objection to a catechist relating with him or her in this manner?"

Professional Conduct for Catechists

Catechists and other staff members must bear in mind that they are professionals rendering a service. Just as a counselor or psychiatrist is professionally bound to avoid emotional involvement with a client, a catechist should strive to avoid becoming so emotionally involved with a student that objectivity and fairness are compromised. Catechists must remember that they have many students for whom they are responsible and who need and may desire the catechist's attention. If a relationship with a student keeps a catechist from responding to other student needs on a regular basis, the catechist should seriously examine the appropriateness of the relationship.

Part 3:

Catechists and Legal Issues in the Administration of Catechetical Programs

TOPIC 1

Handbooks for Catechists and Families

The development and/or revision of handbooks may well be one of the most important responsibilities facing a catechetical leader. A catechist handbook enables catechists to become familiar with the policies and procedures of a religious education program. A family handbook enables students and parents to understand expectations and responsibilities. Each is an essential resource for ensuring that all are aware of program information, guidelines, policies and procedures. Catechists have an important role in the ongoing development of these handbooks — to make recommendations for items that should also be included in the handbooks.

Catechist Handbook

The catechist handbook normally cover at least the following six areas: program philosophy, instructional duties, non-instructional duties, supervision of catechists, personnel policies, and sample forms. Familiarity with all that is contained in this handbook gives catechists the confidence that they are aware of the essentials of their responsibilities and understand relevant policies and guidelines. Often catechists and catechetical leaders together develop a catechist handbook to meet the unique needs of their parish program.

The philosophy or mission statement of the catechetical program is the basis for all policies and procedures. Ideally, the life of the program should be seen as flowing from the philosophy or mission statement. Basically, the catechetical program philosophy or mission statement answers the question, "What do we say that we are doing in this parish program?" Rules and regulations should be consistent with the stated philosophy or mission of the program. It is important, therefore, that rules and proposed rule changes be reviewed in the light of the philosophy or mission statement.

Instructional duties are the ones that are uppermost in the minds of catechetical leaders and catechists. This section of the catechist handbook will deal with what catechists are expected to do in the instruction of young people, delineating some broad guidelines as to what catechists are to accomplish. Other areas of responsibility considered with instructional duties include responsibilities in the supervision of students and records that should be kept concerning student attendance and performance. It is important that catechists be aware of their duties in each of these areas.

The non-instructional duties vary greatly but typically include such areas as supervisory roles on the parish grounds while sessions are being held, off-site activities, expectations for attending parent meetings, etc.

The parish procedures for the supervision and evaluation of catechists, various policies that govern the program and essential forms will also typically be covered.

Family Handbook

A religious education program needs to ensure that both parents and students understand the rules and policies of the program and parish and agree to be governed by those rules and policies. Some religious education programs have separate handbooks for parents and students. This author believes that having one handbook for both parents and students is preferable to having separate handbooks.

The catechetical leader should ask parents to discuss the handbook with their children. In this way, families are able to participate as a unit in the life of the religious education program and parish. Parents share the responsibility for their children's understanding the philosophy of the program and the rules that flow from that philosophy.

When catechetical leaders and other administrators consider handbooks, rules and regulations come to mind. Most administrators and attorneys would agree that the best law is, like medicine, preventive. The best defense is having tried to follow the right course in the first place. Catechetical leaders look carefully at their rules and procedures to be confident that they are reasonable, fair and consistent. Catechists too must keep these norms in mind if they implement rules for an individual group.

As in the construction of catechist handbooks, the beginning point for rule development is the program or parish philosophy/mission statement which is available to all members of the community.

A section on admission policies typically discusses the qualifications and procedures for admission. Another section of the handbook may deal with parish or diocesan policies regarding religious education.

Many problems can be avoided if the handbook states the procedures by which parents contact catechists and catechists contact parents. Catechetical leaders rely on catechists to follow the established procedures.

Catechetical leaders strive for simplicity and clarity in rule construction and long lists of rules should probably be avoided. Phrases such as "other inappropriate behavior" or "conduct unbecoming a Christian student" cover many types of misbehavior. Examples of infractions could be provided. The role of the catechist is crucial in providing for the needs of all students.

Off-site activities, such as retreats and field trips, should also be discussed. If service programs are required, they should be described. The problems of students arriving very early for a program or staying long after a program's end must be addressed. Catechists must be aware of their responsibilities as outlined regarding these activities.

The catechetical leader should retain the right to amend the handbook for just cause and should state that parents will be given prompt notification if changes are made.

For everyone's protection, parents and students should be required to sign a statement such as, "We have read and agree to be governed by this handbook." Catechists can be of great help in the implementation of the rules crucial to providing for the needs of all students.

TOPIC 2

Boards of Religious Education

Religious education board membership is one way that the laity share in the teaching ministry of the Church. What board members do is crucial to the mission of Catholic religious education. It is important that catechists understand the role of the diocesan/parish boards which govern the religious education program in which they serve.

Canon, or Church law, governs Catholic religious education. Catechetical leaders and board members have no authority to act outside the provisions of canon law. But within the provisions of canon law, there is great freedom so long as no civil laws are broken.

Types of Boards

There are currently two main models for boards of religious education: consultative boards and boards with limited jurisdiction. A consultative board is one generally established by the pastor or by diocesan policy. A board with limited jurisdiction has been defined by NCEA publications as one "constituted by the pastor to govern the parish education program, subject to certain decisions which are reserved to the pastor and the bishop." This type of board would have, in both theory and practice, more autonomy in decision making than would the consultative board because the pastor has delegated decision-making power to the board with limited jurisdiction. Pastors and bishops can delegate power, but they cannot delegate their ultimate responsibility for actions taken in their parishes or dioceses.

Role and Responsibilities of Boards

Religious education boards have an important role. It is crucial that board members understand that power is vested in the board as a body, not in individual members. Board members must understand what the role of the board is — the development of policy. Even if the policies have to be approved at a higher level, board members must understand their role in terms of policy.

Policy is usually defined as a guide for discretionary action. Thus, policy will dictate what the board wishes to be done. Policy is not concerned with administration or implementation; that is, the board should not become involved in *how* its directives will be implemented or with the specific persons who will implement them. Catechists are responsible to be aware of all relevant diocesan/parish policies and their role in implementing them.

Parish boards have responsibilities to the catechetical leader. Since the catechetical leader is responsible to the board, as well as to other appropriate parties such as the pastor, the catechetical leader should report to the board how he or she is ensuring that policies are implemented. The catechetical leader keeps board members informed about problem or potential problem situations so that board members will be able to respond in an intelligent manner if they are questioned.

There is no more crucial relationship for the success of the ministry of religious education than that of the board and the catechetical leader. That relationship should foster a sound experience in a Christian community. When the catechetical leader and the board function in an atmosphere in which each respects the rights of the other and in which healthy dialogue and the resolution of differences are promoted, the catechetical ministry of the Church thrives.

A Final Thought

As partners in the religious educational ministry of your parish, you as a catechist have a special role in the building of the kingdom of God. Common sense and prayer are indispensable aids in effective ministry. When facing a legal dilemma, ask yourself, "What would I advise my best friend to do? What would Jesus do?" The answers to those questions can provide guidance in the exercise of ministry that meets both the demands of the law and the imperatives of the Gospel.

Summary Recommendations for Catechists

1. Know what your catechist handbook or other appropriate documents say.

2. Be familiar with the rules and regulations of your program and with any particular rules that your catechetical/pastor makes.

3. Enforce program and parish rules.

4. Establish rules for behavior. Be sure to make the rules known to those affected. Be sure young people understand the rules and the consequences for not following them. Be consistent in enforcing rules. (Posting and/or distributing rules is a good idea.)

5. No matter how angry you may become, never discipline a person without explaining what was done that merits a penalty and allowing the individual some opportunity to explain the behavior.

6. Take every reasonable precaution to insure the safety of those in your care. Report any unsafe building or other conditions to the director or other appropriate person.

7. Do not leave young people unattended unless absolutely necessary. If necessary, be sure that they know what procedures they are expected to follow and/or ask another adult to "keep an eye" on your group.

8. Don't make unnecessary negative comments about young people either orally or in writing. If it is necessary to make statements about misconduct or performance, be sure comments are specific, behaviorally oriented, and verifiable. (For example: Bobby missed six confirmation classes, was late for three classes, and was sent to the director's office for fighting three times *rather than* Bobby is absent most of the time, late the rest of the time, and always in trouble.)

9. If an accident occurs in an area under your supervision, notify the catechetical leader or pastor immediately and write down the specifics as soon as you can.

10. Keep some kind of plan book so that if your professional competency is ever questioned, you will have a written record of what you did and what you intended to do.

REMEMBER:

When in doubt, ask yourself "What would a reasonable person do in these circumstances?" "If someone else were in this situation, what would I advise him or her to do?"

Order Form

Qty	Amount	
____	$__________	*Religious Education and the Law: A Handbook for Parish Catechetical Leaders;* $12 member/$16 non-member
____	$__________	*Religious Education and the Law: A Catechist Handbook** (Each pack includes 10 handbooks)
____	$__________	1-4 packs $20 each pack member/ $26.00 nonmember
____	$__________	5-8 packs $19 each pack member/ $25.00 nonmember
____	$__________	9 or more $18 each pack member/ $24.00 nonmember
____	$__________	single copy $5 member/ $6.60 nonmember

*The Catechist Handbook is designed to be given to catechists, substitutes, aides, board members, etc., for their reference during the year. It addresses the same legal issues in summary form, highlighting the catechist's role and responsibilities.

Additional Resources:

Qty	Amount	
____	$__________	*Making Commissions Work: A Handbook for Parish Religious Education Boards/Commissions.* 1996. 104pp. $15 member/$20 nonmember
____	$__________	*A Primer on Law for DREs and Youth Ministers* by Sr. Mary Angela Shaughnessy. 64pp. 1992. $5 member/ $6.60 nonmember
____	$__________	*Pathways of Faith: The Story of Today's DREs* - Video Cassette. 1994. 14 minutes. $14.95 member/ $19.95 nonmember
____	$__________	Total

Please send your order to:
NCEA Publication Sales
1077 30th St., NW, Suite 100
Washington, DC 20008-3852

or Tele: 202-337-6232
FAX: 202-333-6706

❑ Payment enclosed. (No charge for shipping and handling.)
❑ Bill me. Minimum order $25. Shipping charges will be added.

Name ____

Parish/School ______________________________________

Address ____

City ______________________ State __________ Zip __________

Tele:(_______)______________________________________